5-

What Keeps Us Here

What Keeps Us Here

poems by

Allison Joseph

&

Ampersand Press/ Bristol, RI

ACKNOWLEDGMENTS

Poems from this manuscript have appeared or will appear in the following journals:

The Nebraska Review: "Speculation"
The Kenyon Review: "Dolls," "The Idiot Box"
Onthebus: "Accomplices," "Inquiry"
New Letters: "Endurance"
Ploughshares: "Bronx Bombers"
Cream City Review: "The Sales Pitch"
The Kenyon Poets Anthology: "Territory: Sunday, City Island"
Parnassus: "Falling Out of History"
The Panhandler: "Housesitting"
Colorado North Review: "Faith"

The author would like to thank the following people for their help and support: Jon Tribble, Sharon Joseph, Richard Cecil and Maura Stanton, Yusef Komunyakaa, Carolyn Mitchell, David Wojahn, Garrett Hongo, Ralph Burns, Martha Christina, and Jane and Peter Rutkoff.

The publication of this collection was funded in part by grants from the National Endowment for the Arts and the Rhode Island State Council on the Arts.

composition and design by Ampersand Press
cover design by Merce Wilczek
cover illustration courtesy of Brown University Library.

Library of Congress Catalog Card Number: 92-73325
ISBN 0-935331-11-5
Copyright © 1992 by Allison Joseph

first printing August 1992

Printed in U.S.A.
Recycled paper and soy ink

Published by Ampersand Press, Creative Writing Program, Roger Williams University, Bristol, RI 02809

for Adella Joseph

CONTENTS

I

II

III

I

Speculation

She lies in bed in her boarding house,
    long silhouette against the coarse
      grain of cotton sheets,

Scratchy wool blankets that fend
    off the dense cold of this damp
      country. The pipes overhead

Hiss with overwork, and women
    walk past her door, jabbering
      their island speech, a swift

Caribbean music. Slim, brown,
    no child scars yet, no incisions,
      she hums a small tune,

A melody she can just recall
    from wallflower dances, one step,
      another, a dip then turn,

Dancing a ruse to forget fruit
    and sudden arcing sunlight,
      guava and trinkets

In the marketplace, the white beach
    with its salty crystalline water,
      the one room school, tin-roofed,

Where she learned her lessons
    by rote and pain, the schoolmaster's
      switch biting her palm.

But here she feels the British drizzle
      deepen to rain, shivers, waits
         for her slick-talking bachelor

To arrive, his grin shifty
      and faithless, but so winning
         she'd listen to his lies,

To any story he'd concoct,
      follow him into marriage.
         He wasn't easy, not effete

Like the gaunt movie star
      all the nurses had flocked
         on his release from the ward.

She was the only dark one
      in that awkward gaggle, peering
         at him and his mistress,

A starlet now forgotten. They crowded
      close for autographs, speculated
         about his life, hers—tuxedos, mink—

Though his films were grade B horror flicks
      and no one would remember her name
         in twenty years. The young nurses

Didn't know any better, strained to see
      the jewels nestled in the v
         of the starlet's low-cut gown.

I see her among her gangly classmates
      and want to know her then, to speak
         with her about the slick talk

Of eager men. Cushing posed for more
   pictures, grinning like no movie vampire
      should, released from the dreary wards

Where my mother would learn to handle radium,
   that decade's cure. She didn't know
      its brilliance could kill: all she saw

Were movies full of ghosts, mad scientists
   filling test tubes, their blanched faces amazed
      at alchemy, covert potions changing man to beast.

The Valley of the Shadow

Mornings my mother sang no music,
walked worn tile, efficient,
a woman in need of nothing,

not even her wedding ring, now
dulled bald gold. Her fingers
shaped dumplings from flour

and water, pinched them into balls
she'd flatten with one palm, house
redolent with the stove's kiss

of heat, smell of rising dough.
She'd eat standing up, too busy
to sit when our clutter could

take over, our dishes, crumbs.
I thought she would never need
to be healed, and only rarely

did she come to my bed, chanting
unfamiliar words. She prayed
to forgive, to be forgiven,

psalms a luxury only for this dark.
My mother wanted forgiveness
bestowed upon us like benediction,

and I, sullen, sleepy child,
lay shivering at this voice,
its recitation of the valley

of the shadow of death, a place
so far away I thought we'd never
know it. I lay there, her voice

alive in that dark, a power
I couldn't see, couldn't touch,
but knew, solicitous, quivering.

Penny Candy

Bazookas, jawbreakers, red hots, fireballs.
Their names were a terse violence, a potent
harm, and we craved them by handfuls,

their sugar dissolving on our tongues,
teeth, turning our lips ridiculous blues
and oranges, glucose rampant in our blood.

After school, we'd crowd outside
any local mom-and-pop bodega,
rowdy kids with rough manners,

jostling, pushing, bulky knapsacks
on our shoulders, bruises on our knees.
Afraid we'd shoplift, store owners

let us in one by one, and we held
out our dirty coins to buy Sweet Tarts
and Razzles, Pixi-Stix and Tootsie Rolls,

colored candy dots of pure sugar,
lollipops that grew sharp in the mouth,
cutting pink flesh. We stole change

from our father's pockets, our mother's
purses, digging for dimes and quarters,
pennies and nickels. Every afternoon,

we'd line up outside those neighborhood
stores, fighting and yelling among
ourselves, all the energy of classroom

and schoolyard still with us,
greedy for the taste of sweetness,
for candy bought with bus fare,

lunch money, the sugar we didn't swallow
lingering in traces on our cheeks,
crystallizing on hands, fingers, mouths.

Dolls

for Charmaine

Don't know where you are now,
whether you have children

of your own, whether you wake
at night with a start, still

remembering your handsome,
virile father, a man who loved

new cars, tailored suits,
whose money bought you clothes,

the jungle gym behind your house
where we spent entire days

on seesaws and swings, playing
tag in the yard's lush grass.

I thought you were lucky,
your games and toys, dolls

we crouched to play with,
combing their hair until

bald patches appeared
on their plastic scalps.

They looked nothing like us:
small-nosed, thin-waisted,

figures with blond hair,
long legs. In your room,

door closed, we'd huddle
on the floor with them,

transform all we scrounged
into furniture for their lives—

the cap from a tube of Colgate
became a cup, a tissue box

a bed. We worked hard,
created women whose bodies

were wanted by the blank
plastic flesh of the male doll—

dressing them in ribbons
and bits of lace, painting

their faces with watercolor.
Not knowing how life came,

we banged male and female
together, while outside the door

your mother and father screamed,
voices hot with accusations,

his strong black hands throwing
plate after plate at her,

at her small, terrified body.
We played while the screams

went on, while your parents
shook in their anger, china

smashing on the kitchen floor.
All I know is that you moved away,

fleeing with your mother, leaving
the house I thought was beautiful,

your handsome father alone,
the swing set out back, rusting.

Accomplices

How else to know our bodies' secret selves
but to undress in that damp room,

a basement far below your house
that always comes back to me dimly—

white wall panels, linoleum tile, a bar
for your father's liquor. That day, we barred

the basement door, stripped down to pure
shivering bodies, girls wanting to be women,

shamed instead by skinny, ashen legs,
hard chests just relieved by nipples,

or baby fat—plump arms and thighs,
the slight, preadolescent swelling of stomach.

You were the one whose body
had let you begin, who first felt

her warm blood seepage, who stood before us,
stripped to belt and pad. Was this why

you coaxed and teased us naked,
so we could fill with an envy

we hadn't known before, didn't understand?
I don't know how much you knew

about the body. More than I did, certainly,
you had brothers and they had magazines

with naked women posing in them,
all tousled hair and lace, their skin

a furious pink of arousal.
Four brown skinned young girls,

we stared at those pages, not knowing
sex's thrust and shudder, just this

glossy by-product. It would be years
before anyone would lift me onto his hips,

entering me and not that girl,
a child who refused to love

her slow, shambling bones, gawky overhang
of clavicle, years before she'd slick

on lipstick, wear high heels.
It would take so long

before she knew sex as wholly hers,
able to grasp whatever flowered

within reach, press it to her lips
to taste and touch, pare down and back.

After Touring the Public Rooms

Neck stiff, mouth a thin line,
I stare at the camera

my father points at us,
my mother beside me,

smiling shyly, my face
pinched, inscrutable.

We've just finished a tour
of the White House's public rooms,

their decor fussy with sofas
and china. Sentimental, fifteen,

I'd like to think I'm someone
special, capable of feeling

melancholy as something almost
palpable, so I don't smile,

sullen on the package bus tour
we've booked, its fifteen

minute stops at the Lincoln
and Washington Memorials.

I am learning to write poems,
fascinated by the crumbling

brownstones we pass in our car,
the train yard near our budget

motel. Standing next to my
lanky mother, a woman

patient with her glum child,
I don't know how good I've got it.

She's all limbs and fingers,
collarbones and cheekbones.

I do recognize her calm though,
crowd close as if I could

absorb it, wanting
to be like her, despite

my notebooks, the half-born
poems I wouldn't let her see.

Later, when she grew ill,
I wouldn't embrace her sickness,

no longer thinking loss a luxury,
no longer enamored with the ways

in which we lose, our lives grown
smaller, more authentically painful.

Creed

In the sickroom, one grave male voice,
free from static, radio hiss,
recites Scripture chapter and verse:
    You will not fear the terror of the night
      nor the arrow that flies by day,
    not the pestilence that stalks in
      darkness,
    nor the destruction that wastes...
My mother listens, head bent
to the glowing dial, hair finer
now, thinned from chemo, x-ray.
Clutter of illness crowds the room,
tired chaos—cups and plates, tissues,
brown vials of colored pills labeled
DANGER, EXPERIMENTAL. I bring water,
food, leave it on the bedside table,
next to her bulky Bible, her notebooks
filled with scratchy exegesis, notes
on redemption, revelation. She wakes
and sleeps to hollow echoes of choirs,
testimonials of reformed sinners,
their born again voices calm, so solemn
I think salvation must be erasure,
damage effaced by the Word's power:
    Let not the flood sweep over me
      or the deep swallow me up,
      or the pit close its mouth...
They speak of Jesus easily, certainly.
Christ is merciful, the Lord good.
Diseased, my mother's lungs are dense
with stealthy cancer cells dividing
among healthy ones, swarming like sin.
But she must believe the body can mend,
the ragged come clean, like the addict
who now preaches the gospel, his voice

coming through the wall to my room,
its calm too delicate, too perfect.

Limits of Imagination

for my mother

Easy to imagine you, newly arrived
    from Canada, walking the wards,
      long, dim corridors of Bellevue,

stethoscope curled around you neck,
    a small thermometer, silver-cased,
      in your hand. *A nurse always finds*

work, you said—early shifts, late shifts,
    double duty in ICU, Emergency.
      You trudged up the stairs of our house,

and I helped you undress, slipping
    the soft-soled white shoes from your feet,
      hose curling around your ankles.

Easier still to imagine you at Keener,
    far from the city on Randall's Island,
      walking the grounds with Robert Chow,

the Down's Syndrome boy you loved,
    always asking what he liked best to eat.
      I see you bend to hear his answer,

his hand pressed in yours, head tilted
    to meet your eyes, your beaming face.
      In Harlem, at Manhattan Developmental,

you had the plain, practical stuff
    of healing at your hands: gauze,
      liniment, antiseptic to clean

the cuts and scrapes of retarded children
    who fell after running too fast, trying
        to chase some ball or toy.

You'd hold them as they cried
    a loud, difficult primal cry,
        whisper to quiet them as the sting

set in, and the pain held.
    But to conjure you, thin, weak,
        leaning on my arm to walk the ramp

at Sloan Kettering takes all I've got,
    all the concentration I can
        gather without pity, or self-pity.

When I try hardest, I can remember
    your appointments at Radiology—
        you'd trade street clothes

for a thin green gown, lead vest,
    and they'd fire x-rays at your body,
        trying to stun what thrived

in your lung, breeding there heedless,
    dividing without caution or care,
        more reckless than I could ever know.

Endurance

I am tired of metaphor,
the lure of the tragic
making me turn the shadows
beneath my mother's eyes
into words like *sullen*
gradations of light.
I should say this plainly:
a woman, dying, seeks God.
Say that she travels to Israel,
traces the routes of Jesus
whispering ancient names:
Judea, Galilee, Capharnaum.
She stands on stone the color
of fine sand in one photo,
near a frothy slip of water
in the next. How my words
turn her life to conjecture,
uncertainties I can't answer
in phrases, poems. I can't
tell you how she felt among
young Israeli soldiers hoisting
her scarred arms, the chemicals
that stunned the spots of cancer
in her lung. But I want
to conjure something
like a street bazaar,
where my mother picks up stones
from a vendor who speaks
a halting pidgin English,
holy stones washed in the river
Jordan. He'll show her a vial,
call it holy water, and she'll
buy it, wanting blessings to hold,
own. But I can't tell you what
it's like to be born again,

to rise incorporeal in prayer,
loving He who has died and risen.
I can only guess the dust
of that country is nothing
like the dust here—the thin
translucent film clouding
my photos. Can only say
I'm tired of distance
of the studied calm of words.
I want something real
as a woman with a Bible
stopping to rest while climbing,
sitting on rocks to read
from Revelation: *Then I saw*
a new heaven and a new earth,
for the first had passed away
and the sea was no more.

At That Moment

I wanted to be there with you
at last, to smooth back your skin,
touch your mouth, eyes, hair,
caress your fine forehead.
When the call came, I sank

to my knees, needing to cry
the inconsolable cry of one
who has waited, the receiver
loose by my ear, clattering
against the wall. I did nothing

until some strong arms carried
me back, holding me as if
my life had become precious
in the loss of hers, as if
they could keep me from it.

They put me to rest
in the narrow dorm bed,
my room now strange, unfamiliar,
and I didn't want to claim
its books, clothes, neat piles

of papers. I wanted to know
nothing of chemo, of IVs,
of the long hours you aged
and withered: waiting rooms,
doctors, experimental drugs,

pain killers. All I wanted to be
was your daughter, the girl
whose hair you'd struggle with,

comb snagging in the coarse mass.
You fought to tame it, pulled

a pressing comb through snags,
my hair sizzling with heat
and oil. You'd try to hold
me still, careful to keep
the comb's heat off my scalp,

neck, my hair now slick,
straight enough a regular
comb could glide through.
You'd braid it then,
two ponytails held tight

by elastics, barrettes.
In our cramped kitchen,
you knew nothing of illness,
strong fingers able to grasp,
hold, braid and weave.

From a Household

we got by, we got by,
Lord knows we got by.
                    Al Jarreau

I
Old clothes become rags, grocery sacks
double for trash, and the Sunday paper,
once read, lines what we wish to protect—
under sinks, in closets and cabinets.
In this house, the ordinary lives twice,
forced into service until spent,
tattered from the urgent work
of fingerprints and dirt. We tire what
we live with, exhaust box springs and
mattresses, cushions and chairs, our
furniture sagging to accommodate
our bodies' changes—paunch, girth,
growth spurts. Such taskmasters,
we make everything serve us
until it runs down, caves in,
eroded from our tread, our damage worn
into carpets, chipped onto bannisters,
spilled on linoleum—our stains and scrapes
paling as we age, growing nondescript as scars.

II *Mother, sewing*
Ceremony of cloth, of thin
translucent tissue patterns

pinned to the yardage. Her long
calloused fingers cut each piece,

allowed for seams and darts,
deft with the heavy scissors.

Scraps and swatches—poly-cotton,
nubby wool—drifted to the floor,

the carpet. She kept an old
candy dish, filled it with

needles, eyelet, rickrack,
thread, bobbins, buttons,

intricate machine parts.
Loyal to all ends, she tried

to save swatches in grocery bags,
but they clung behind sofas,

chests of drawers. Later,
on hands and knees, breathing dust,

I'd sweep under chairs, in corners,
loosen what she'd left behind.

III
Each year we'd take it
from its disintegrating box,
unwrap it from a dusty

plastic bag—long pole
of splintering wood, fake
fir branches, metallic

red stand. We'd piece together
our tree's grand illogic,
try to make its parts look

like trees hustlers were moving
out on cold street corners,
some of which burned, unsold.

In that season of the new,
we hauled our homely tree
up from the garage, blundering

to match right branches
to right slots, fitting
them in, pulling them out.

We dressed it in tinsel
bought the day after Xmas,
in lights that glowed,

then burned, wiring frayed,
plug loose in the socket.
We opened our gifts

in that dim corner, folded
the wrap, though we didn't
use it again. Days later

I'd find thin silver strands
all over, proof of blessings
in our lovely, shabby house.

IV
Elegant, smoothly curved,
the blue Mercedes sedan
sits stalled in our drive,
stopped from my father's
hard use. I can't remember
when last it moved, but know
the wounded blue interior—
cracked leather curling
from the seats, door latches
speckled black with rust,
its faded brass nameplate.
When I'm home now, I touch
the aged torso, remember

the pull of its tires as
it took the road, my father
speeding in unabashed luxury,
though we were only going
to market, ripped coupons
in our hands.

V

One look at Van Gogh's sleepy, heavy-headed flowers
        and I'm back in the house of my father's incompletions,
its half-painted rooms fathomed in the silence

between sales calls and bills, income and orders.
        But it wasn't just Van Gogh—a miniature
town of Constable's hung on the dining room wall,

a pastoral mass-produced, yet still somehow
        exquisite—spume of a turning water wheel,
aged house and barn in deep green, mud brown.

And it wasn't "Waterlillies"—no, instead
        my father gave us the huge swath
of a field by Monet, a woman and child

enveloped by lush grass, the woman holding
        a parasol in one hand, the child
in the other, marking her territory, claiming it

like a prize or gift. He bought heavy vases,
        porcelain—scarlet tanagers and redstarts
perched on boughs, painted on that smoothness.

Oh, he tried, in our house of odds and ends,
        for some beauty, tried still when the oven
would not close on iron hinges, when tiles

36

he had cut so carefully came loose from caulk,
    breaking to blue shards in the bathroom.
Father, you did not know how to keep

that house from coming apart around us,
    would not admit anyone could do it
better—so wallpaper peeled on old

edges, bannister rails loosened and fell.
    Still, you loved the circus scenes of Toulouse,
put Degas' dancers on our walls so they could

stretch, bend, whisper songs to one another,
    titter behind cupped hands.

VI

Looking under sweaters, stockings, garter belts,
    I find the album, "Our Wedding" etched
on its white quilted cover, ribbons and bells
    engraved around the words' swirling script.
Again I had to dig it out, turn its pages, yellowed
    translucent paper between each photo,
protecting this man, this woman. I know the lists
    of guests, stare at the bride's dress
of plain lace, her pointy heels, gauzy veil,
    at the groom's tight jacket, baggy pants.
Over and over, I come back to this album,
    try to convince myself these faded pictures
have something to do with me, that my limbs
    came from their limbs, those lives.
And now I recite their small events, flesh
    out the fine details, places the camera
blurred, unsteady, left something lost.

II

Trying to Remember: One Trip Back

Weeds and alleys, gullies of rainwater,
    chalk drawn against sidewalks,
        hopscotch, rhyme and chant
of jump rope, sky tilting down, full
    strength of sun, glass fractured
        to glitterings, cracked pieces
in the sewer, the block one small row
    of two stories, uneven lawn patches
        marking one from another,
late model Fords and El Dorados rusting
    in driveways, salsa and Spanish
        late nights on AM, teenage
Puerto Rican and Dominican girls chatting
    together about boyfriends, older sisters
        nursing boyfriends and husbands,
late evening click upon click of dominoes
    high and low tremble of voices—Jamaica,
        Grenada, Trinidad, Barbados—
a long syncopated calypso shuffle, one foot
    following another into dance, wild growth
        of open lot across the street,
fallen branch, twisted root, rock and boulder,
    no paved land, garbage dumped
        illegally each night,
wild cries, stray dogs howling until dawn,
    dim daylight opening my eyes each
        brittle winter morning, early
walk to bus stop, black stench of bus
    exhaust, crush of schoolkids, loud
        voices, awkward bodies—
skinny elbows, ashy knees, torn hems on skirts,
    the schoolyard's flat black asphalt,
        the building a looming fortress,
spiked iron rails, chain link fences, plaster
    ceilings and splintering wooden chairs,

one voice booming discipline
over the P.A. system, words learned rote,
lessons, tests, chalk against blackboards,
another language, calmer here
than on the streets, words aloud, chanted
in unison: *libro, cuaderno, lapiz.*

Bronx Bombers

In a way, athletes die twice. We die the day our careers
end; we are usually young men when that
happens. Then we die again, finally, completely.
　　　　　　　　　Lou Pinella, *Sweet Lou*

Those seasons, fans showered Reggie with his own
candy bar, cheered a team with the slick defense
of Craig Nettles, so effortless at third, baby-faced
Ron Guidry, a hot accurate flash of Louisiana Lightnin',
and Chris Chambliss, the sanguine veteran
who trotted easily around the bases,
as if this game didn't really get you anywhere.
On television we watched Billy Martin
storm out of the dugout to kick dust on umpires,
while Steinbrenner roared from the front office,
spitting threats at Reggie, whose likeness

was everywhere those days—print ads, commercials,
on the free t-shirt I got when we crossed the Bronx
for "Reggie" day at the Stadium. My father refused
to go to the ball park unless there was a promotion,
some gimmick or gizmo being given away.
So I got a plastic batting helmet
which I wore in the hot stands
all one home game, while a young boy behind us
declared he was there to catch a ball, pounding his glove.
With that pennant race so strong, it was easy
for my father to pretend I was a boy,
to buy me a souvenir program that listed
the players' full names, ages, lifetime stats.
From where we sat in the park, though,
they were only small figures, no superstars.

And when it seemed a game was irretrievable,
my father would storm out, angry his money
didn't guarantee a win. I followed, headachey,
sour taste of chewed pretzel in my mouth,
sound of vendors hawking beer and hot dogs
in my ears. Listening in silence to the radio's
postgame show, we crossed the borough again,
passing tenements and bodegas,
storefront tabernacles and beauty parlors.

Today I don't follow the game.
Thurman went down in a plane crash
and they became a team without a captain
or catcher. They wore black arm bands
all the next season, mourning incongruous
with rowdy fans. The Mets are the team
to beat in New York now, though Steinbrenner
still harasses his players.
Those old World Series teams have scattered,
divided by trades and retirements,
though Guidry is still on the mound,
just a little edge off his fastball.
He still kneads his glove in that tough way,
working the leather. My father, widowed,
sits on the edge of his bed,
rubbing his aching shoulder,
working it, grimacing, face contorted
like Guidry's into the wind-up:
a twisted look of effort, then release.

The Idiot Box

"But can it core an apple?" Norton asks Kramden,
another get rich quick scheme of theirs
gone awry. This time they peddle knives
on TV, as if they could ever sell enough
to get Norton out of the sewer, Ralph
off his bus route. This late at night
almost nothing's on but reruns—
Lucy bawling after Ricky, *The Odd Couple*
clashing, Spock and Captain Kirk
on the flimsy set of the Enterprise.
In his room, my father snores gently,
asleep despite the TV's glare, its volume.
He's even got the radio on—classical—
I don't know how he sleeps.
Awake, I stir at the sounds
of wind in the eaves, mice skittering
between walls and floorboards.
If I turn off his set, he'll wake, protest,
say he was watching whatever was on.
So I lie in bed in a house
where four broken sets haven't been thrown away.
One black and white set belonged
to my grandmother, a woman pale enough
to pass, miserable unless she watched
Lawrence Welk—the old couples
dancing wanly in crepe and polyester,
the chipper cast singing show tunes.
The only black man on it
dances a happy soft shoe, lithe.
When my father wakes, he'll rise, shower,
run his hand over stubble, razor bumps,
a few clumps of hair in the sink.
He'll put on a suit, a dark one, tie
and cufflinks, spend days trying
to sell what he's got going—plots

of Florida land, local real estate,
specially printed business cards.
As he dresses, game show hosts give away
money for the one right answer, and
my father has it, laughing at greedy contestants
on shows where the answers are simple enough
anyone might win, light up the scoreboard
for a split-second, that fraction
it takes to hit the buzzer.

Yard Work

Late summer, the crabgrass of our front yard
high, spiky, concealing rocks, shreds
of paper, candy wrappers blown to bits
by winds pausing to rattle our house,

to rattle all the small brick homes
on this cut-off street where I grew up,
watched my friends grow up, leave from,
disappearing somewhere beyond these houses

I haven't seen, having left and returned myself,
perpetual daughter. Tall weeds, my father set
on pulling them root and stem from earth,
the lawn mower burning, spitting

new-mown grass from its side,
tough stems I'd rake, or heap high
in my arms, straining to carry heaps
of underbrush—rotting branches, twigs.

Shirt front wet, my father calls for water
laden with ice, belly swelling with mid-age.
He's out of breath, tired in full sun.
Foolish enough to fight this land in summer,

we use fists and forearms to clear
ragged weeds, debris, the scaly rocks
underfoot, will leave the yard razed
almost a new habitation, something

we'll survey with one eye shut,
assessing our good work. But right now,
my fàther calls *water, water,*
an old cry, one not yet obsolete

with insistence, or angry demand.
Upstairs, I'll fill a pitcher brimming
with ice, hold it tight between sweaty palms,
so no drop's wasted, not one drop spilled.

The Sales Pitch

for my father

The garage is all yours, full
of overstocks you couldn't move,
ditched here for no one, not
even me, nosing around on a
Saturday. It's dark, but not
so dark I can't find the pots
and broken planters, the bags
of gravel and moss and soil.
Out of business, you liquidated
coleus and cactus, sold ferns
to close one store, another. No
rational reason why I'm here,
just my need to see your life
before me, its object still
freed from the hard sell.
So I pick brochures
off the floor, now dirty, once
glossy with shots of Florida—
lushly leaved palm trees,
women walking blue surf,
a deserted stretch of beach.
For years you talked homesites,
communities, monthly payments,
cities you'd only seen tapes of—
Malabar, Vero Beach, Silver Shores—
names as beautiful as profit.

In a rented room, alone
with file cabinets and phones,
you tried that urgent talk:
My friend, never will there be
another opportunity like this
you've got to buy before the prices rise...

You said you'd work for no one
so no one helped when rent
came due, when the phones
went dead. Those phones sit
slack in their cradles here,
the cabinets rust unopened.
Father, this is the only way
I can look at your life,
the way I can believe
your sales voice is gone.
In *Salesman's Opportunity,*
another order blank waits
for you to fill it, another
no risk trial offer—
greeting cards this time,
or mail-order jewels.
You could unveil them
a piece at a time, just
one sweep of the hand—
palm up, fingers poised.

Territory: Sunday, City Island

My father drives the City Island strip:
Italian restaurants, bait shops,
antique haunts and seafood joints.
He tells me they're all Mafia-run,
this isn't where blacks should be
come night. Controlled territory, turf,
but it's late summer, daytime,
the light and season keep us safe.
     At Johnny's Reef Restaurant, we sit
outside at wooden tables, eat lobster
from plastic trays, splitting boiled red bodies
with our fingers, mine no longer clumsy,
knowing how to crack the body, where
the shell hides its meat. Around us,
a pre-Labor Day crowd buzzes: girls
in lace Confirmation dresses pose
for roving photographers,
a steady stream of cars flies
the single starred Puerto Rican flag,
boom with salsa, merengue.
     In hours, I'll be back at school,
my father giving me up, surrendering
to his schemes: Lotto tickets, gambling,
as if he could win, buy himself out
of the noisy, thumping Bronx.
He prides himself on this dinner, though,
pleased at how I open the claws,
suck out the meat. Such things
give us satisfaction today, solace
months after the cancer took my mother,
withered her small and gone.
     I look at the grimy water,
the barren stretch of coast
fenced off from the restaurant.
My father sights pigeons, and I turn

51

to see him grasp one whose claw
is caught in wire and string,
his face almost as steady
as in the photo of him in Grenada,
young, a policeman, just out of his teens.
His voice, whispering patience,
takes me aback, makes me wonder
how many creatures he's held this way,
how many others he's shown this tenderness.

Heartbreaker

My town's beer and pizza joint
is one long shaky bar, a few
scattered tables and chairs.
My friends and I come here early,
before restless students descend
to punch scratched oldies on the jukebox,
swig from long-necked bottles.
We're students too, but trusted regulars,
familiar, especially to the men
who don't ever seem to leave,
though they've got stories—wives,
damaged crops, prison wards, parole.
One shows me a picture of his nine year old,
doesn't know where her mother went.
Another asks if I know who Jaco Pastorius was,
how he died, humbled and bleeding,
outside some Florida nightclub, beaten
as if he were no one. My girlfriends and I
watch out for each other, knowing
what a miracle of affliction
these men can be, especially
when they don't hide what they want,
like this one at the bar yelling

She's got a great ass, his face
sun-damaged, eyes red, narrow,
hands thick with dirt.
He repeats it, and I flinch,
knowing he wants to touch me.
But I'm untouched myself,
know little of seduction,
and I try to ignore his noise,
the smell of beer on him.
The hands that will comfort him
are the ones that drag him home,

53

try to wash off the alcohol,
peeling back his jeans and shirt
to bathe him, run a cloth
over stubble, a thatch of hair.
If it's me he wants, he'll have
to learn to love himself, to soap
his body down in gestures
of respect, washing silt
from his skin. I pretend
not to hear him, listen
instead to the jukebox's trill,
Jagger singing *Angie*, voice
drawing the name out in ache.

Rationale

Think of a moon the color of jaundice,
a sky so dark I rely on streetlamps,
the neon signs of all night diners.
Alone on the streets tonight,
I work my way through the din
of several foreign languages, past
the Korean market where an elderly man
washes fruit with a coiled green hose,
oranges and melons cooling in the trickle.
Music pumps from the Tip Top Lounge,
thump of oldies amid the bump and grind
of beer glasses—Martha Reeves belting
nowhere to run, nowhere to hide,
her voice tight with need—

I know you're no good for me,
but free of you I'll never be...
I stand outside your fire-singed tenement,
trace scrolls of graffiti on its brick.
The lights aren't on in your place,
only tall girls—stilettos, short skirts—
linger out front, call to men passing by.
This night, humid and simmering with noise
recalls the days when all you wanted
was the cold sliver of my body, pulling
me to you with a force that left my wrists
red. I drew my nails down your back,
traced the groove of your spine
as you slept, woke you to kiss
arid lips, tight skin.

Now we're nervous memorabilia:
letters, cards, one pressed flower,
colorless. Wanting you, I'm skittish,
quick as a hand of three card monte.

Inside your building of few windows
flicker with old movies, black
and white romances I once searched
for clues. But there's no plot here,
no scheme of grief and release.
Inside, you might be turning in bed,
sheets wrapped round your waist, torso
bare, lungs filling and contracting
the same way they did our thousand-odd nights.

Family Life

The couple upstairs can't decide
whether to break it off. Her sobs
come down to us, spectral,
continue longer than anyone
should cry. He sounds surly,
but we can't make out his words,
can tell they hurt her, petty
for all they've lost.
They make me think nothing's safe,
that one day I'll walk into
my apartment, find it all broken
or gone. They make me think
no one's ever safe, not my mother
at the sink, hands in suds,
turning to deflect my father's
quicksilver anger, his temper changes
so sudden he'd soon try to hold her,
though she'd want none of the embrace.
His anger, fleeting like the money
that didn't pay our bills,
returned, eventual testimony
to our house, his loss.
Her funeral was near his birthday,
and he leaned over, said,
So this is what your mother leaves me.
Better this, I thought, than to be
fighting still, squabbling over
money, religion, utility bills.
I keep hoping the woman upstairs
will leave, hoping she'll rise,
spine straight, eyes unaverted,
walk right out his door, down
the stairs, out of his life.

For a Godmother

Your eyes made me think you were lonely,
    the pallor of your skin distinct
      among our darker browns, our blood
      untaxed by sickle cell. I hardly knew
you, can just recall your gaunt, sad face,

its bones pushing up under pale skin
    like something unrelieved. We took
      your few things home after you died:
      a black and white TV, some 45s,
and I wonder if you ever danced alone

to the records, drifting through ballads
    and blues, dreaming of hands that would
      touch the delicate nape of your neck,
      the slick between shoulder blades.
Or did you take someone in your arms,

lying with him on sheets stolen
    from British hospitals, wards
      so far from this city, this New York?
      Your few relatives were here, your
goddaughter a surrogate child, although

I don't think you ever held me, wonder
    if you were strong enough to hold
      anyone, your blood cells bent double.
      After years, your face comes back
to claim me, to remind how fragile

we can be, our lives suddenly over.
    But tonight, I'll forget
      the errors of your body,

the forces that made you faint
on our stairs. I'll imagine you

weren't alone in your dark rooms,
      your mouth kissing clavicle, shoulder,
       each bone of the ribcage, hands
      sliding down to kneecap, shin,
ankle, pleasure trickling down

nerves to each limb, finger, and toe,
      your pulse growing as you touched
       and were touched, all of you
      alive, heady and warm,
down to the pores of your skin.

Falling Out of History

> *The rage of the disesteemed is personally fruitless, but it*
> *is also inevitable: this rage, so generally discounted, so lit-*
> *tle understood among the people whose daily bread it is,*
> *is one of the things that makes history.*
>
> James Baldwin

On TV, the friendly pickaninny
wags his head, dances a buck and wing,
so black the whites of his eyes
bulge as he rolls them back.
Damn cartoon, I think, as my cousin,
age four, does not move, watching
this prancing boy loll his head.
I thought this was behind us, past tense,
like separate fountains, lunch corners.
Still, in the language, it's *black magic,*
black widow, black-and-blue.
At twelve, I wanted to control it,
lured to Woolworth's messy aisles
by cheap perfume, eye shadow, rouge.
With effort, I could be pretty,
fade myself into one polished certainty
of skin, until I didn't offend, not black
but something I couldn't recognize.
My mother would close a wet thumb and forefinger
over my nose, hoping to narrow it.
Nothing changed. Phillis Wheatley,
country of origin unknown, came
to America at seven, by thirteen wrote poems,
at twenty wrote: *Some view that sable race*
with scornful eye: "Their color is a
diabolic dye." I open the paper, read:
Slavery brought blacks here to share
in the country with the greatest opportunity
on earth...a man in Michigan calls racism

unfair, asks *Would anyone know Cosby,*
Jackson or Murphy if they were born in Africa?
Phillis wrote: *I, young in life, was snatched*
from Africa's fancied happy seat—her nation's curio,
the forward to her poems signed by eighteen
famous Massachusetts men. Finally freed,
she died alone at thirty-one, obscure
in a run-down boarding house.
It's all buying and selling, I think,
try to divine what Phillis knew
beyond pious couplets: *Remember, Christians,*
Negroes black as Cain may be refined and join
the angelic strain. I can't guess much,
my language not falling easily into couplets,
breaking down when I examine it, the concept
of race as actual and arbitrary as anger.
My cousin, bored now with the television,
wanders away, content to push
his fire engine across the floor,
slowly, intently, inch-by-inch.

Broadside: from Decade's End

after the death of Yusuf Hawkins

My sister calls from back east:
another black man shot
for the company of a white woman,
another dose of anger in her voice
as it travels long distance.
Soul and race may be private
dominions, but everyday she feels
another infringement, sees another
network special on the perishing
black family—Bill Moyers repeating
didn't you know, why didn't you use
to a young black welfare mother,
a girl who sleeps with her babies
as if they were younger sisters.
As we watched, each
in separate cities, east
and midwest, the same cleft
of anger rose in both of us,
the same contempt for network
moguls who thought this necessary,
who sent cameras to pan Newark's
downtown storefronts, its projects,
where boys, if lucky, make it
from adolescence to manhood,
knife blade of violence so common
on those streets. But anger isn't
anything we haven't already known—
as schoolgirls, we were a credit
to our race, not like others
who mugged or robbed, wish
fulfillment for administrators
and admissions officers—both
woman and black, but skilled,

able to talk white.
First day freshman year,
I saw two other black faces,
was dumbfounded later when
a roommate asked, *What's lynching?*
her eyes lifted from Malcolm X's story.

Nothing and everything
has changed, and there's
nothing like fear or rage
to make the self shut down.
Still, I have Zora and Nella,
Sojourner Truth baring
one black breast, insisting
Ain't I a woman, Billie
crooning *love*, her voice
cutting a silken swath.
And I am far from what
my sister calls war zones:
Bensonhurst, Howard Beach,
old enclaves of white hatred,
tradition of yelling *nigger*
at any black who ventures in.
And I wonder how far we've come
from Emmett Till's eager face
maimed and gouged, his mother
mourning in public, another
casket lifted onto the shoulders
of sisters and brothers.

III

Immersion

Each day I swallow a tiny pill
to turn my body against itself,
shut down its tubes and nodules
so nothing's released, so no egg

travels its slender circuits.
At night, no modesty conceals
our skin, and suddenly we're

conscientious as children first
forming cursives, straining
to stay in the lines. We touch
calmly, as if skin could burn,

peel easily back as paper,
tense with love, the air humid
as if with contagion, or worry.

Riot rides beneath our skins,
deep where I cannot reach
to take it apart, our bodies
difficult as daylight.

I hold you all the harder now
having read today about the pill:
no researcher can tell me

whether or not in twenty years
a dense lobe may take hold
in my breast, hard as the gyn's
metal stirrups. Certain of only

our union, I ride you faster,
conscious of this deep immersion,
this clench of jaws, arms, hands.

Meditation at Month's End

These days each month I grow heavier,
breasts rounder, balloon-like,
though this body's no carnival,
no gaudy music, flashing strobes.
It's estrogen, progestogen,

one pill once daily, regimen
to keep the body in place,
just as I am placed under you,
rooted tight by grasp, grasping,
nothing like angst near us.

I wake to your cartography of scars,
hum and scent of breath, your skin
a braille of hit and miss: mole, pore.
And when you loom above, cresting in,
it isn't anything like falling,

nothing like pity or pathos.
It's you, one more trial of flesh,
one more bodily refusal to cease
living, give in. And that's the moment
I know we're mortal, our hopes

false as forgery. That's when I know
all we want is not to wither, not
thin into gossamer, unconfined
by delicate manners. Sure,
we've got soft touches: tongue,

palate, fluttering eyelid.
But we hunger after solid mass:
muscles of calf and thigh, bodies

beaded in sweat. Today, I'm pendulous,
swollen to the body's limit, the mind's.

Take me as you would any excess:
sparingly at first, testing, testing,
then drink, taste, know we can retreat
to our own sumptuous illogic, hold off
any cold and shuttered face.

Preservation

The man I love washes in my shower,
soaping, rinsing his body's slopes,
hair slick on his forehead, neck,
water scaling his broad back.

I wake to his sounds this morning,
close my eyes to envision him
beneath me, urge and push of sex
still not familiar, something

I've learned needs patience, accuracy,
one deft maneuver an apex of pleasure,
or sudden, sharp pain that unhinges me,
leaves me more open than scars,

than our mouths when we kiss.
He asks what I feel, and I
cannot answer, cannot find one word
to describe the efficacy of touch,

the grain of his skin enough
to make me want him always,
to touch him as I've never
been touched by anyone else.

Joining him beneath the spray,
I run my hand over his soapy
stomach, then down to the groin,
sliding between folds of skin,

spreading lather on thighs, knees,
calves, then let go to set curves
of breasts and hips against him—
water and sweat mingling, his tongue

a strong, solid taste in my mouth.
I want to feel him harden, so I'll
send my tongue deeper, move his hips
with mine, take him wet and whole

inside, our bodies saving us,
keeping us here just one moment
longer, one moment that opens
and closes, like a mouth or fist.

Inquiry

How does it feel as you
pull this body to you,

move mouth over breasts
whose tips flare, angered,

flesh that refuses consumption,
rebels against you, closes up,

off, as if you could do nothing
to appease its want, its demand?

How does it feel to take me—
skin and muscle, blood and cuticle—

lips pressing yours, your hands
stroking a glissando of spine

quivering as you slide into me,
swollen, haughty, aware of how

much you'll lose? I could not
be you, spilling yourself

in me, each spasm of coming
a 'small death', as you told me

the French call it, would not want
to die each time in roseate folds

of labia; to labor, stiffen, groan
with such roughness and tenderness

you cannot look at me, at anything
in the room, but instead close

your eyes—halcyon, magnificent,
breath coming quick and tenuous,

a line of expiration tying you
to this world. No, I could not

have taken me—eager, wanting,
full of trust—and laid me down,

not for rest or sleep, not
for anything but these negotiations,

these entrances and exits, this body
loaded with decline, its past

of sloughing and redemption,
its present boding nothing more

than this continued and continual dying,
proceeding each day like nothing unusual,

nothing you'd call extraordinary.

No Ways Tired

One long draught of kindness,
your weave of skin over bone,
arch of your worn body.
True, we sag, give way,
skin aging, hair aging,
face each day's
immutable evidence of loss.
But I'm no ways tired
moving with you—soft clefts,
curved back, private trails.
Celebration and honor.
We have no meager parties,
no slight get-togethers,
loving until we're proud,
the world's benevolence
shining through. We love
so much our image stays
with me, and I close my eyes
to summon you—fingertips,
lips, chin and chest—
litany for my church,
my sanctified evening,
when the phone, rocking,
won't bother us. Let it ring.
Let mountains rise. Let our bodies
continue their distinct story
of touch, caress, strokes
of sure hands, rites
to keep us live, growing.

The Swath of Afternoon

Today you teach chokecherry, bramble,
    show me clusters of frosted hawthorn,
trace their sharp scallops of leaf-edge,
    showy pink-white flowers. Its dry fruit,

like small mealy apples, will later,
    pitch a dense weight to forest floor
at just a touch, a shake of branches.
    By a stand of Eastern white pine,

you stop to let its needles prick
    your fingers, kneel on a bed
of loam and green slivers, livened
    by cones, by scales of mossy bark.

Even in this state park, where each
    stint of trees is labeled by species,
and wooden plaques, neatly lettered,
    tell us what we gaze at, you're happy,

able to locate, discern, matching
    guidebook illustrations to living bark,
unfurling flower, the blaze of leaves
    saluting the air—black oak, red oak,

the rougher slippery elm, which you say
    grows from sixty to eighty feet,
inner bark sticky with a juice
    once used to ease sore throats.

Tree of healing, I say, only a little
    mock pretense, loving that this earth
could cure, restore, offer up a salve
    trusted in folk wisdom, pure belief.

I take your hand, not just to feel it,
    but to hold it to this tree, so we
may note its quiet legend—red-brown bark,
    notched leaves, pods like tiny wings.

In Fear of Sleep

Humble in slick skin, you lie exhaling
to night, air weighty as new coins,
your limbs heavy in sleep. In lack

of light, your face is artless,
a random blur, and I touch
breath-mist, chapped skin,
the rises of your features.

But when I lie with you,
I can't help think danger,
disaster, apnea the reason

you might not wake—your breath
stopping dozens of times
throughout the night, heart
thudding to keep you alive.

I may seem frail, but it's
you who fights, who could
blink away before I could

do anything. Tied
so slenderly to this life,
you breathe and struggle,
twist, turn, as if you

could easily give up,
enter a land where peace
isn't the rare rest between

moments, but the quiet exactitude
of your body no longer wearing

itself out. All I wish for you
is a merger of body and breath,

hours where sleep means rest,
rest means calm, and calm means
more hours here, in my tired arms.

Learning the Blues

for Jon

You taught me testimony,
slow-dragging the night until
our mouths kept time together,

arms around each other,
silhouette huge, rocking
silent on the wall.

Nothing to that dancing,
one foot forward, other
back, pulling me closer

as the music grew, growled—
thunk of Lightnin's guitar,
Willie Dixon's sinuous pleas,

I just wanna make love to you
sung over and over, sear
of love undone in his voice.

Lights down, just one bulb
glistens mid-ceiling,
furnace rumbling the house.

I've got you close, under
fingertips, near enough
to lick salt off your neck,

for you to whisper all about
Slim Harpo, Koko Taylor,
Sonny Boy's porkpie grin,

and Bessie's sweet shimmer,
all that woman loose upon us,
her holy, holy voice.

Housesitting

This house isn't ours but we dare
to make love in another's bed,

cries blanketed by shut windows,
an electric fan's cooling hum.

Owning nothing here but humid skin,
a few summer clothes, we borrow

this life, a trial of work
and marriage, rise early to

insistent mewlings of cats,
appliances in the kitchen waiting

to whir or chop, for us to claim
that hope of home. So orderly,

this house invites us to long
for life this good—rows of books

neat on their shelves, photos
of all we've loved under glass.

And I want it, want it like bread
or your body: a clean, settled place

where any ghost of mine is welcome
to hitch up under the eaves and stay,

where you may spend hours figuring
moves on a game board, reading rules,

rolling dice as luck unravels,
moves you forward. What could move us

forward, slide us into a future
with our lives wound one round

the other, our names almost the same,
your hands tucking sheets on a bed

large enough for both of us,
room enough for sleep or lust?

We turn older in the ache
of decisions and deliberations,

our thoughts one sort of union,
our linked bodies another.

Anticipation: for an Unborn Child

Before the day they pull
you from me, I'll read my old

biology text, remember the hours
of cells vibrating under low

and high power, magnification
from specks to whirls of motion.

I'll chant each name, a litany:
vacuole and centrosome, nucleus

and mitochondria, words stately
yet still scientific, mysterious

enough to describe all the flux
in us, all I will build in me.

I'll think of the hours spent in lab,
dissecting frogs rank with

formaldehyde, the model
of the body we studied as if

we could will it life, the liver
blue, spleen red, the chilly

plastic parts heavy and smooth
in our hands. Slides and stains,

tissues and organs—all will
make sense to me—all layers

of the dermis, Watson and Crick's
spiralling DNA, amino acids

tight in their templates—
will matter as much to me

as the morning of your conception:
a clear unbroken stream of sun

shining into the bedroom,
the grainy skin of your father.

He'll enter me and you'll begin,
the world in all its delicate

detail will matter—pistil, stamen,
mitosis, osmosis. Burgeoning

in me, not yet whole, a name
not yet spoken, you will

take all I have to give, grow
from the single slim membrane

of egg to the blastula's fierce
cluster of cells around space,

an embryonic world so alive
I will move as it moves, hold it fast, strong.

Late Letter

for my parents

I'm tired of us, faces so alike—
of lip and brow, oval brown
eyes, foreheads high and regal,

of our history, the past we share
secondhand, its solo movies replaying
behind my eyes. You were once young,

once beautiful, full of promise
as you leaned on a fence in a country
I never saw: uncreased, eager

newlyweds, arms around each other,
one continent and two countries
ahead of you. But what do I really

know of how you spent your days—
silence, speech, questions unanswered?
I'd like to think you were happy,

loving each other with something
like passion, greater than need.
But from each photo, questions:

how did she feel in that dress,
caught in his arms, did he ever
whisper her name? What buzzed

inside your heads at the sight
of one another—her limbs still
gangly, his face unmarred by failure?

All you've left are questions,
dogged as any new wife. You've
got me cornered, waiting on proof,

managing from memory. Still waiting
for the visitation of your voices,
the good looks of your youth, both

of you sharp, slender; lives open,
untold, ready for me to come
and question it all, unraveling

anything akin to myth or story,
wanting behind the facade of sepia, photos
faded before you could tell their truth.

Faith

Small, swollen, heavy in your hands,
my breasts rub together, thin skin
chafing. You have taken this body

in, as I have taken yours,
given me your mouth, your hands,
the catepillar crawl of your fingers.

This is power, I think, power
to give, to give to, acknowledging
pockets of pain, days of ease

and forgiveness, when we think we shine
like no one else, your hips sliding easily
against mine, a new bump and grind,

shimmy, stroke, jelly roll. I want
to believe this is prayer, the body holy
even in daily losses, to know this even

of my mother's slow and eventual
dying, her body still hers, not lost
despite the pain, the weaning away.

I still see her face in faces
of thousands of black women;
their high, smooth foreheads,

precise cheekbones slanting
under vigilant eyes. Brown gloss
over hips, thighs—I am released

knowing their bodies curve
like mine, grow gracious, wise,
ample of this journey.

What Keeps Us Here

Who wouldn't claim this nighttime
meeting of fingertips, my body
fused with yours, yet so

distinct, so utterly separate?
Who would dishonor us, call us
foolish and headstrong in our ache

for each other, our heady lust
contained in these bedrooms,
in all the rooms of our future?

Light spills in pinpricks from above,
fake stars, phosphorescent, glow
over our heads, a fixed universe

some previous tenant devised,
as if the quivers of light
the real sky pulses forth

were not enough. Soon you'll sleep,
close your eyes to drift
through its uneasy thoroughfares,

its way stations and islands
of dream, terrain where your footing
slips, balance sliding out

from under you. A lunar scape,
cloaked in ice, where no one
speaks your name, or rouses you

from the planetary chill.
Who wouldn't want then
to hold another before sleep,

to grasp a stay against
the turning, changing world,
its wide, uncharted legacy.

Allison Joseph was born in London, England in 1967 to parents of Caribbean heritage. She grew up in Toronto, Canada and the Bronx, New York. She holds degrees from Kenyon College and Indiana University. Her awards include the Academy of American Poets Prize, the Ruth Lilly Fellowship, and an Associated Writing Programs *Intro* Journals Prize. Her poems have appeared in such periodicals as *The Kenyon Review, Ploughshares, Parnassus, New Letters* and *Crazy Horse*. She lives in Little Rock, Arkansas, with her husband, poet Jon Tribble.